A Clear Mind

A Clear Mind

One Man's Experience of Life after Lymphoma

ROBERT TOSEI OSTERMAN

iUniverse, Inc.
Bloomington

iUniverse books may be ordered through booksellers or by contacting:

iUniverse
1663 Liberty Drive
Bloomington, IN 47403
www.iuniverse.com
1-800-Authors (1-800-288-4677)

ISBN: 978-1-4502-7928-4 (sc)
ISBN: 978-1-4502-7929-1 (ebook)

Printed in the United States of America

iUniverse rev. date: 01/10/2011

To Dan Kammer

We are what we think.

All that we are arises with our thoughts.

With our thoughts we make the world.

Speak or act with an impure mind

And trouble will follow you

As the wheel follows the ox

That draws the cart.

…Speak and act with a pure mind

And happiness will follow you

As your shadow, unshakable.

Buddha (*Dhammapada*)

CONTENTS

Preface

There is no pain without joy, or night without day. There is no Death without Life.

In 1995 I experienced my mortality, that is, death. I became aware that someday I will cease to exist in this physical form. I do not recall that I had a sense of fear or a feeling of dread. I felt that I was merely an observer who watched the symptoms and the therapy that was taking place in my body.

In March of that fateful year, I was scheduled to have lower back surgery in order to repair a slipped disc. During the pre-surgery physical examination, the lymph node in my left groin was found to be swollen. After a biopsy, I was told that I had lymphoma. After another biopsy of a swelling under my left arm, a culture from my throat because I was losing my voice and the harvesting of bone marrow samples from my back; it was determined that the cancer was localized in the groin area.

This diagnosis was followed by four months of chemical therapy, four months during which time I felt that I was approaching the doorway to death. I had sores in my mouth, but this did not matter because food tasted like tin. At times I had difficulty breathing, and was once admitted to the hospital and given a three pint blood transfusion to increase my white blood cells. I also had to give self-injections for the same purpose. After each treatment, my urine was blue in color, which I thought was funny. Injecting the chemicals into me became an adventure because my veins suddenly turned shy. My digestive system was in chaos, and my energy was at a low point.

The chemical therapy was followed by eighteen treatments of radiation therapy. Compared to chemotherapy, radiation was a snap. A sunburned groin and a burnt lower colon were not pleasant signs, but at least I was able to eat food again.

Following radiation therapy, I had the lower back surgery.

During the summer of 1996, I experienced my immortality; that which never dies. Many names have been given to that which is Everlasting: the Fundamental, the Unformed, the Spirit, the Mind, and God. Yet, to quote Lao Tzu, an ancient Chinese sage, "Experience is beyond the power of words to define...."

As a result of these two experiences, I realized that all life, all that exists, can be seen as mortal and immortal. Here is Lao Tzu again,

"...Words make then seem different only to express appearance. If name be needed, wonder names them both: from wonder to wonder existence opens." (*The Way of* Life)

Each existence was alive as in a fourth dimension perspective. This occurred when my mind was cleansed of impure thoughts.

A Clear Mind is a memoir of my observations of individual existences and of my thoughts, and my ongoing practice to purify and calm my mind through attentiveness. I know now that a pure mind is able to see all things in their beauty and wonder. I also began to sense that a purified mind brought me real freedom: freedom from clinging to life and freedom from the fear of death; this only happens when I sincerely apply my self to my practice. I understand that this is the most important thing that I can do in my life.

My daily random observations were recorded in a notebook. I have rearranged them under ten themes in order to bring some structure to this book. I begin in the winter and spring of 1997 with new and pure minds, with innocent life: the small children who rode on my school bus five days a week.

I am grateful to everyone who helped me during that difficult time and to all who offered favorable comments on this work since its inception. Thank you Allegra Wakest for typing and editing the text.

All that is written herein is my responsibility.

Tosei,

2010

Wonder is the conception

Of anything wherein

The mind comes to a stand.

Spinoza, *(Ethics)*

Chapter 1: A School Bus And Its Passengers

When I make half turns, my signal remains "On."

We look so funny in our big boots, as we kick the defenseless snow.

Our teacher wears white stockings and sometimes white socks too.

Today she wears her baby blue snowsuit. Her name is Samantha, but she calls herself Mantha; she is always happy with a smiling face.

It is difficult to see if the windshield is covered with snow.

Right now, "There's mom's house" is her national anthem.

My kids, my bus, and me; we sing *Jingle Bells* on February 3.

Children always walk in the deep snow instead of on the path—and joyfully.

The red stop sign stands in the cold air.

The air is bitter cold, the bus is sweet.

They smile when I call them Mr. M and Miss K.

The yellow ponytail holder is returned to Mom.

An invisible companion: diesel fuel on my gloves.

She held the Christmas present in the palms of her hands as if she was cradling a newborn puppy.

A slow engine becomes sluggish, too fast, it burns up; slow, it sees not enough, fast, it misses much.

The crossing guard wears an orange and yellow vest and a red cap.

We pass a field of dry cornstalks.

If you want to be a child again, ride around in a busload of them.

My bus makes no right turns on red.

When we stop for new riders, we flash our warning lights.

The overhead mirror reflects the little people.

We always help friends up and down.

We put on our flashing yellow lights and stop at all railroad crossings.

A pre-trip inspection is done every day.

It is easy to see why we are attracted to children; they have great potential.

In the morning Ryan wants to be called Justin; in the afternoon Samantha wants Kate's name.

"Mother and father are people; grandma is people too."

When I drive my bus, there is movement outside; tranquility inside.

We merge onto a busy freeway.

I have a cut on my thumb; so one of my pre-school passengers said, "Take medicine, put on band aid." So when I arrived home, I put on some antiseptic ointment and a band aid. This is called Wisdom.

We're crossing a busy intersection.

There is a lot of traffic on snowy days.

Kate said, "She's a girl, just like me."

CHAPTER 2: WINTER SCENES

Snow flakes: little worlds floating down.

Today is a grey, cold day; crows are crowing.

The snow falls like mist upon the white ground and the snow-catching pine trees as night approaches.

The strong west wind carries the snow across the road.

Snowflakes fall and touch my dry lips.

The tree still carries its ashen-colored and dry leaves, but some have fallen.

Snow rests on a shaking pine branch.

Icicles come out when the sun shines.

The snow-colored smoke disappears into the grey sky.

There is a tiny scent of spring in the air today.

After a calm day, the wind blows.

Here there are many bare trees leaning on the afternoon sky.

Ice forms again after a warm day.

The ice on the pond is melting, but animal tracks remain.

The water runs beneath the ice and down the street.

No gloves are worn now, but hands still in the pockets.

The harsh and damp east wind comes from the cold lake.

The trees still have red ribbons on them.

The top of my beige car is white today.

These are the days of the long march to spring when each new storm, each new snowflake, adds to the weight of winter.

People are unhappy when the snowfall amount exceeds the forecast, but they are happy when forecasters are too generous.

When a heavy snow falls, life catches its breath.

We worry about the roads when they are lost in the snow.

It is true what the song says, "On a clear day you can see forever."

On a partly cloudy day there is sky and there are clouds.

An east wind brings clouds.

The clouds in the distance are like the remains of an artillery barrage.

The ice is leaving the shore.

Today is a winter day of rain; tomorrow, four to six inches of snow are predicted.

The snow is really blowing.

Dawn brings dark clouds under a blue sky, and the first glorious, golden rays of light.

There is a pink sky in the east, a full moon in the west.

All of the trees are white this morning from the wet snow.

Slowly, the snow is falling from the trees.

A slight breeze causes the snow-covered and leafless branches to shake.

On a foggy day the world is a dream.

The pine trees are delicate and beautiful in the fog.

I learn a lot while walking around in the fog.

The cold wind blows on my head.

The moon is trying to hide in the blue sky.

A Clear Mind

The trees are reflected on the surface of the still pond.

"The mist dampens my clothes; the rain soaks me."

The wind interferes with the pond's stillness.

Chapter 3: Home Life

My wife says that she's feeling hemmed in, "Let's go somewhere, do something; but first, wash the bathroom floor."

The fire in the fireplace is out. The turning fork rests on the stone hearth.

We make love in the dark under the covers on a cold night.

Each morning I touch the alarm clock.

The woodpile on the deck is sheltered against the cold.

Sparrows rest on Super-bowl Sunday: a quiet day.

In the dark I listen to the water softener.

The pink carnation in its clear glass vase has lost its smell.

I worry about the pilot light on the water heater.

I prepare the coffee at night, and in the morning it waits for me.

Ten years I've had a wife; I've forgotten the single life.

The vacuum cleaner, with its little light, can't decide whether to push or to pull.

A cup of coffee leaves behind a perfect ring.

One bottle of beer is enough to put me to sleep.

The water drips repeatedly in the water closet.

On a sunny day there are many shadows in the basement.

Spiders live in the corners of the basement.

There are three trees and I sit beside them.

On dark stairs I know where to step.

Not knowing the clock, strange is the ticking.

I push the buttons on the telephone and they sing to me.

Even the coffee filters need a place to rest.

Sometimes we leave our lights on during the day.

The telephone rings only once.

The coffee maker makes a lot of noise after a quiet night.

When I tap the red recycling bin, it makes a hollow noise.

Someone picked this banana especially for me.

When I look at a picture of my granddaughter, I am happy.

The cat catches mice in her dreams.

Once people have been killed, they should be brought to life. This is called make-up sex.

My wife says that it is a small thing to put down the toilet seat.

My thoughts stop when the furnace goes off.

My wife said that the style of men's shorts changed after The Boxer Rebellion.

I read return addresses on the mail.

A drooping plant is held upright by a wooden stake.

Little seed pods on the floor: is Mr. Mouse here?

My wife has a stiff neck. I told her that she's carrying too many thoughts. She doesn't believe me.

Chapter 4: People and Places

I like a bagel with jam, a cup of coffee, and a place to read.

The waitresses wear blue and white dresses and speak Spanish like missionaries.

Pancakes with syrup so big I cannot see the plate.

When two women talk, one always nods her head.

A nun's clothing is called a habit.

The bride wore a white dress; the groom wore a black tux.

Teachers in a school are called the faculty.

A woman wears a chartreuse dress and brown wool leggings.

Workers are laying stone to the sound of music.

The fire burns the superfluous parts of the new house.

"Bake bagels in small batches."

Potatoes in the slicer are sacrificed for french fries.

Germans eat sauerbraten and dumplings.

When the doctor told me that I had lymphoma, my whole life turned surreal.

The lady wears a purple cap, and she has one arm.

Teenagers are too serious.

With old eyes her face is young.

The restaurant is full of teenagers and a lot of chatter this morning.

After the arrival of the cake, one feels so humble.

Today is Ash Wednesday; people have ashes on their foreheads.

I once cut a monk's scalp while shaving his head.

Luxury is contrived; can it be the Way?

Opulence smells musty.

The music, music, music never stops.

When the pneumatic doors open, I pay attention.

The five-star resort hotel has a garden.

When I see a simpleton, why do I call him that?

I see a very tall man; and at the same time I almost fall down the escalator.

Two old men, twins, with the same grey hair; they wear identical tan coats.

I feel the braille dots on the plastic coffee cup lid.

My teacher is an obstacle.

An impossible task: being a teacher.

In North Dakota I can see a long way without obstructions.

The large jet is very quiet as it approaches the airport.

Every human being is a wonder.

Can I learn to live as if I'm on vacation?

A vacation helps me to realize life's endless change.

CHAPTER 5: ANIMALS

There is a hawk on the top of a bare tree, and there is a mouse on the white snow.

Beneath the grey sky geese hack and flap at each other.

Animal tracks in the snow wear a path from tree to tree.

Crows cry before sunrise.

Two ducks float with wings spread.

A blackbird walks on the white snow.

A squirrel, his tail flapping and flying, crosses the street.

The little birds sit like commas in a row on the telephone line.

Geese glide in the atrium of the mall.

A squirrel shouldn't be undecided in the roadway.

Two birds are flying like mad.

Birds frolic; spring is near.

Geese soar way up there in the blue sky.

Each morning animals go to and from the pond.

A dog barks across the field.

A bird flies past the window.

Suddenly I see three blue jays on a birdfeeder, and my emotions accelerate.

It seems to me that birds migrate with the prevailing winds.

Unlike geese, when I go with the wind, I worry about the return trip.

Sometimes the geese fly high, sometimes low; it depends on the clouds, and the sky.

Two doves huddle in the rain.

A low flying hawk lands on the lone bush in the prairie.

The hawk, white breasted, sits on the branch like a monk.

Patient, watchful, quick, and graceful like a hawk are good qualities.

Maybe a hawk needs more than one marsh in which to hunt.

The hawk doesn't mind the rain.

Geese in v-formation are flying south.

Today the ice is off the pond, but a single quacking duck floats near the shore.

A lot of ducks and geese are on the pond today.

A chickadee hops in the grass on the outside of the window.

Plump robins avoid flying.

Life is so difficult, but the squirrels and rabbits don't complain.

All of a sudden there is a cardinal.

Many ducks with wings pumping fly in circles.

The hawk is not in the snowy meadow today.

A black cat is hunting in the farmer's field.

Two geese, a small bird, and a breeze are on the pond today.

The ducks and geese seek shelter near the shore.

Chapter 6: Observations

I love these small books, the ones with few words; they slip easily into my breast pocket.

In the dawn light I skip a page in my notebook.

My car's engine drones as it warms itself.

I read aloud the words in my books; they feel better when they hear a human voice.

I often think of cutting back on my reading; this would be like cutting back on my breathing.

The lonely flag on the pole waves to me.

From the hilltop clouds float on the horizon.

A poor person knows silver from junk.

To live in tradition is to lick my stamps.

The telephone poles are holding hands.

If the universe was not a vacuum, where God would put things?

Underneath we're identical; but we're also different.

Too many things soil my touch.

There are no heels on tube socks.

Words often tumble out of nowhere.

If I want someone to learn the Way, I have to be an example for him.

Dusk prepares me for the night.

Getting dark, that's what it does.

It is peaceful when I am in the only car on the road.

Dust settles on the table without effort.

When I go to a chiropractor, I am manipulated and well adjusted.

For a time I was afraid of the dark, but now we are friends.

Tall road signs approach my small car.

How can I know where I'm going when driving a fog?

My headlights show the way in the early morning.

My favorite candy is bittersweet.

Pasting slogans onto paper is ambitious.

Sometimes there is an airplane in the sky.

When I live in a backpacker's tent, I can touch the roof.

Are conservatives too rational?

Should I be disappointed when the coffee is cold?

I am feeling bogged down; I need to do more manual labor.

Sunrise is such a glorious sight: gold and grey clouds.

An airplane in the sky leaves a vaporous trail.

Sumatra flavored coffee is bitter.

A purple and pink sky is growing at sunrise.

Every now and then, I bite my tongue. I wonder about this.

The flag is torn by the strong wind.

When I want to have a good laugh, I classify people by the shapes of their noses.

The brown vines on the fence obstruct my view.

I should change my name every few years.

When I travel with others, my pace changes in order to accommodate them.

The lawyers for the defense were called "The Dream Team."

How to lose three days: turn my watch calendar from Feb. to Mar.

Today there is no flag on the flagpole.

When it's dark and quiet, it's time to rest.

The first kite of spring has crashed into a tree.

Words and phrases have their own distinct flavors, like chocolate and cinnamon.

I try to care for all things because nothing lasts.

I've looked into it: everything works for awhile; nothing works for very long.

A walk in the woods is helpful.

When I do something stupid, it often turns out to be humorous.

To remain hidden is best.

It's so easy to stay on top of the comfortable tracks.

The black hole has always been there.

There is an old Chinese saying, "When the wind blows, all the blades of grass bow their heads."

A spaceship is not required in order to arrive in space.

The Hale-Bopp comet is a mesmerizing sight.

Sometimes there are dips in the road.

CHAPTER 7: ZEN MOMENTS

Early in the morning I sit in meditation by myself.

After lighting the candle and the incense stick, I bow to the wall.

"The art of life lies in a constant readjustment to our surroundings." *(The Book of Tea)*

"The essence containing all flavors is the supreme delicacy."

Zen Master Fenyang, *(Zen Essence)*

There is nothing to say while the incense stick burns; saying nothing, the incense stick burns.

Sitting in meditation is the outward sign of my mind.

I am the steering wheel; the steering wheel is me.

The very best way to live: without effort.

I live on the bottom of the ocean where everything is connected.

To be without effort is to put aside efficiency.

The ocean's view: it gives perspective.

"For those who arrive on the Way, everything is 'it.' This power is very great."   Zen Master Foyan (*Zen Essence*)

Some Eastern philosophies say that all things are unreal. What better reason is there to treasure them?

There is one match left to light the candle.

Life is a riot with all of us fish swimming in the ocean.

The Way: the Way is open, unobstructed. That's how the Way is.

When I follow the daily schedule, the night is effortless.

I wanted to be a Zen Buddhist monk, but that was long ago.

The bright moon shines upon the empty birdhouse like wind through a flute.

I am like a sponge attached to the ocean floor.

To actually see myself is quite a leap.

Practicing in sleep, I fall asleep.

I chant prayers after meditation.

The music passes through me like air.

In the midst of luxury there is peace.

Avoiding evil is like seeing a pothole in the road and driving around it.

"The Buddha is the creation of our own mind." (*Teaching of Huang Po*)

"...Make the changing appearances of the springs, rocks, plants, and trees through the four seasons into meditative work. This is how wayfarers appreciate the landscape." (*Dream Conversations*)

Lao Tzu's *The Way of Life* calms the mind.

My teacher said to me, "Make your wife happy." An impossible task was my thought. Now she remains unhappy, but it's not impossible. I've learned, "Yield and you need not break." (*The Way of Life*)

Another teacher said to me, "Stay at home." What did he mean by this?

A sage does what cannot be done.

Sheldon Kopp wrote a book, *If You Meet the Buddha on the Road, Kill Him!* If you see the Buddha while you are washing the dishes, kill him again.

Sometimes sitting in meditation is a hindrance.

I like my practice to be comfortable; I'm afraid when I don't get enough sleep.

Sitting in meditation is one of the many, many expedients that point the Way.

I thought that where I held my hands during meditation was important, but that was like sitting with my thumbs over my eyes.

To live in the transcendental hurts my eyes.

To realize my errors and ask repentance is the Way.

After finding the Way, why do I want to put it in a barn?

An old adage: do what is required in every circumstance.

I wish that I could just do what I'm doing.

The religions of India, China, and Japan did not espouse causes or crusades.

To be truly a person of the Way, I need to be a trick rider: getting on and off at will.

Following the Way is to be sincere and to be natural.

I stick to the path that I have chosen; it is most likely the right one. I don't let anyone talk me out of it, not even myself.

More, more, more is not the Way.

Using strength is not the Way, but wholeheartedness is the Way.

My teacher must pass away also.

In the bathroom there are three mirrors. If I stand in front of the center one, I can see three images. Who is the real one?

That's an intriguing term: "The post-Zen Era."

Chapter 8: Body

My ridge-topped wool cap is crushed down, and my face is unshaved. I wait on the down escalator as others rush past.

The cuffs of my gloves curl up and show their dirty linings.

The sound of my watch: hhmmmmmmmmmmmmmm.

When my heart skips a beat my hand trembles.

Sixty winters have I seen, not much left to talk about.

When the hearing goes, I've heard enough, and when the eyes go, I've seen too much.

I have more gas the older I get.

My clothes have many pockets; I often lose things.

When I pull the shoelaces too quickly, they get knotted up.

Would I miss my hat if I could not find it?

When I die, the world dies also; when I close my eyes, what is there to see?

Birth happens in a flash.

Death happens in a flash.

What can be without being?

If I could see me on my deathbed, I could make great progress.

What exists is.

Why is it that I'm trapped in this unending dance of pain and happiness with death as the only outcome? Is this truly the degenerate age?

Time and space are conditions which allow me to meet others.

Everyone should watch another person die.

Whatever I'm doing, whatever my plans, whatever I own, death takes away.

Nothing is under my control, not even how I shall die.

A stop-watch stops time.

Without time life is timeless.

I just eat the food that is available.

I learn something when someone close to me dies.

Often, death is a lot quicker than birth.

Yet, I spend a lifetime waiting for death.

What is my most precious thing? Am I willing to die for it?

How can I be better than anyone else? I've lived just like all others for sixty years.

When I hear how men die in this age, I wonder what has happened to the human heart.

As generations before me have passed away, mine is next.

Perhaps the term "passing away" is better than the term "death."

Causal elements combine and there is function: the wind blows over the water and there are waves.

To stay alive and to put out is the game.

There is truth in the old saying: keep your head cool and your water warm.

I do something, and then I die; I don't do something, but I die anyway.

The lag between impulse and action can be reduced to instantaneous.

Here are a couple of questions I ask myself: how many breaths do I take in a minute? Can I take ten breaths without losing track of my counting?

River all around and walking with friends is the Greek Way.

There is no time when I am sleeping.

My life is like a drop of water sliding down a windowpane.

It is easy to slip on the ice.

Far-seeing is to take in all things.

I should watch each thing like an egg ready to hatch.

It is true: to lose my life is to find it.

To live in the world is to be one with the world.

I do what I can, and then I die.

It's about fear, and the great matter of life and death.

"There is no difference between the quick and the dead; they are one channel of vitality." (*The Way of Life*)

I'm like a blip on life's screen.

Birth and death are serious matters. Laugh at birth and death.

CHAPTER 9: MIND

Thoughts come and go; it is best that I just watch them.

My mind wishes to be anesthetized with thought.

When a baby cries does he have the thought, "I'm hungry?"

Before I was born did I exist in God's consciousness?

My thoughts are like vapors in a room.

Whatever is my mind makes it so.

Briefly, anger darkened my mind like a sudden snow shower.

I bend the words to fit the form, twist thought to fit the habit.

My mind is like a revolving gear.

Mind is the natural way.

Can I be conscious of nothing?

I relax when my mind is alert.

When I am angry with someone, it is usually with me.

It is not a matter of getting better, but of understanding.

Stillness and activity: mirrors of the mind.

The mind is the house of birth and death.

If I listen to me, I know what to do.

Sometimes my mind is closed like an old rag that the wind blows against a fence.

If I could understand that every existence has an end, then every thing and every person would be precious.

I'm waiting to see what my mind has to say.

With an open mind the impossible is possible.

Pride keeps me from helping others.

I always know what I'm doing.

What could be more interesting than my mind?

It's amazing how readily and easily my mind grasps any little slogan, comparison, fine distinction, or whatever.

An open mind often has a corner in it.

If I see the "Who," the watcher of my thoughts, my view is blocked.

Every illusion is closer to a solution. Socrates' answer was, "I know that I do not know."

When I see the full moon, my thoughts disappear.

My old mind forgets more than it remembers.

Finding the Way is like trying to remember a name which I have forgotten.

To follow the Way is to remember where I put it.

As long as I think there is a difference between weekday and weekend, there is a difference.

I thought that not everyone was able to realize enlightenment, but I was wrong.

How subtle and quick are these subjective assessments.

Bowing opens the mind.

I am myself when my mind is open to all things.

Ego is my thinking mind.

Doing God's will is an open mind.

When I try to form a concept of the universe, I am unable to do so because I'm in it.

If I want to teach, I have to be patient.

Even a sudden insight leads me into the woods.

A baby, crying for milk, doesn't think about it.

My smallest thought can bring forth action.

It is necessary to slide off the pyramid of my beliefs.

There is nothing I can teach others that they do not already know.

Love is being open-minded.

I want to write about systems, but I don't know what to say.

It is easy to grasp a slogan.

My mind can be captured by Buddhism and Catholicism.

There is a subtle difference between contemplation of oneness, watching the breath, and a free mind.

The one who speaks first catches the other in deep thought.

Deep in thought is to be far away.

To have an open mind is not to be in outer space.

With an open mind thoughts wouldn't think of appearing.

A Clear Mind

To be humble is to put aside my thoughts.

I think that only a fool is spontaneous. I protect myself.

When I draw pictures of my thoughts, I am surprised.

I am more firmly conditioned to some things than to others, money, for instance. These are called hot buttons.

I'm amazed at how easily I am hooked on a desire for fame.

Does experience lead to knowledge?

My mind often runs amuck.

I want to discipline everything except my mind; it can wander off and do whatever it wants.

I do it all of the time.

Thinking stops automatically; no need to stop it.

To live in my mind is to die in my mind.

I respond to many false signals.

I need to learn to let go of my mind.

My mind cherishes every event, every word that it thinks.

To be a good athlete, I need to forget my mind.

This is a hard step: mind.

Use it without putting any label on it.

To "let go" doesn't mean to throw away.

I once thought that luxury was an obstacle to the Way. This was caused by my closed mind.

And how many centuries do I think that I have to live?

Where do my thoughts come from? What a stupid question.

Sometimes I give voice to a few words in exchange for a little fame.

Alcohol and drugs quiet the mind and eventually kill it.

My mind is upset at the slightest deviation from the regular schedule.

There is one Mind and one Self. My individual spirit is the self, the wave; original Self is the ocean.

Everything that is is in the Mind; what cannot be enlightened?

It is not a matter of gaining original mind or losing illusory mind.

Everyone wishes to give Job a literal interpretation; yet, The beginning of *the Book of Job* is clearly allegorical: it has to do with Job's mind.

Oftentimes, I have been reconditioned by Scriptures.

My conditioned mind was created during many years of work, like a granite block that is slowly carved into a pillar.

Is it possible to have a clear mind 24 hours a day?

When I live in my head, it's impossible to get over my thoughts.

Polishing a stone does not produce a tile; polishing the mind, thoughts continue to arise.

In order to avoid pride, I consider that everyone appreciates a sunrise.

The sword that kills is a conditioned idea.

The sword that liberates is an open spontaneous act.

One of the pitfalls is the "discipline" of the head.

Today, I lost my checkbook, and my head.

There is mind; there is mirror. This came to me in a dream.

To do this right, every word should be carefully considered.

Religions cite scripture, give lectures, and provide moral precepts.

An open mind is just the natural way.

A thought without passion dies quickly.

Do passions precede thought?

In the blink of an eye, right understanding wipes out a thousand things.

I am a concept in Mind.

The brain and its impulses are thoughts and air.

Brain impulses are conditioned.

I am amazed at a baby's first word and its continued use, forever engraved on a little brain.

With concepts a baby is conditioned to like and dislike.

Free from grasping thought is enough.

Is the brain a "clean slate" at birth; the Original Mind?

Waiting for thoughts and ideas to filter through from my Big Mind is called wasting my time.

It takes a lot of energy to hold these 10,000 conventions and conditions in place. Space and time alone are tremendous burdens.

A Clear Mind

As death approaches the grandfather of my children, thoughts increase, and also remembering the past.

Thoughts without emotion are easily disposed of.

Can I approach death with an open mind?

Each day I am more convinced that all answers are within.

Thought is also transmitted from mind to mind.

Transmission from mind to mind occurs regularly.

Trying to hold off thought is a lot of work.

An open mind lets thought naturally flow through.

It is really nothing until my mind recognizes it.

Consciousness is a concept.

I have to let go of my prearranged speeches.

My passions are programmed into me.

Poetry is open to all possibilities.

Mind is a concept; open mind is a concept too.

Energy is expended not in the thinking, but in the holding on.

First, there is open mind, and then thought, then open mind, then thought….

Conditioning is so subtle that I forget from day to day.

My thoughts are like bubbles in a glass of champagne.

Everywhere I turn there is another slogan, another cliché.

When I remain tense, thinking has me.

It's so easy to get stuck on something.

I'm trapped once again in these subtle dualities.

The great battle of life and death is fought in the mind.

Once I get a song in my head, it's hard to turn it off.

My mind is like a mirror with legs. Saying this, I walk through a puddle.

I often get attached to the words that I read.

I spend much time in games of gain and loss.

There's an old saying: if you own nothing, then you own everything.

It's easy for me to get sentimental—feeling mental.

Whenever I begin to generate fear and uncertainty, I'm hooked on something.

When I see a great light, I try not to get on it.

Falling into everything seems to be my thing.

Life is a series of little red lights.

It seems to me that fear of life increases thinking.

Thoughts come to me, and then they leave me.

There are no thoughts to still; I only think there are. Thoughts pass through me.

True thoughts are unborn and do not die, what about clouds—or anything?

When I keep a clear mind, life flows.

I am so possessive of my thoughts; it is as if I own them.

There is nothing between me and the entire world.

Once I've been there, I am free to return "to the ashes."

Everything in the universe has Great Potential and Great Function.

Fear increases thought, which isn't necessarily negative.

There is a beautiful transmission when a good hitter and a good pitcher look into each other's eyes.

I'm careful not to get hooked on my teacher's proverbs, or my own.

If I have some success, I have a long way to go.

I see the fundamental in a dream.

After I have travelled far, what need is there for books?

Longing for peace and quiet, my anger rises.

Old habits are subtle.

I could fill up half a book with a list of my old habits.

It happens—just about the time I give it all up or after my fifth cup of morning coffee.

I realized that nothing in my life had to change.

I receive insights all of the time, but I'm too busy to recognize them.

With one giant step, I've been there; but then I left. Now I know how to get back, but I can't make it in a giant step.

After many months in the cave, there is a new moon tonight.

I don't throw away anything: form, awareness, not anything.

My dreams show me the way; therefore, I push on.

Dear Tosei, With great anticipation, I read your article "What is Dharma?" Alas, what a bunch of junk, strictly Buddhism 101. Great was my disappointment. My head ached even before I had completed it. Sitting in meditation with shaved head is supposed to cool the mind, not act as an incubator.

When nothing remains, then there is the fundamental.

The case: stopping thought!

"Light overcomes the darkness."

To be enlightened is to wake up and understand waking up.

Now is the grunt work... seeing in 40 days, or 20 years?

Even if I should die before teaching another person, it is OK; I'll come back to teach.

It is a great help to have a clear understanding of illusion.

I become a wave in order to understand the ocean.

My mind is like a boiling cauldron cooking up a thousand demons.

There is no thought; there are thoughts; there are no thoughts....

If there had been no one to keep it alive through the centuries, could it somehow survive?

No thinking equals interconnection.

When I'm serious, I'm probably thinking too much.

The final word should be: "I don't know."

If I see a bird and do not know its name, it is best that way.

I am always looking for a thought upon which to hang my hat.

If I go far enough, two options appear: reality or illusion. Both are the same: nothing or something—or both! That is what I do! I give rise to the play, to whole worlds.

Here are two questions: can something come from nothing? Where do thoughts come from?

CHAPTER 10: PURE MIND

Realization is like this: Twelve of these, ten of those, six of this, four of that, three, two, one....

A pure mind is ordinary.

I pay attention when walking down an ice-covered driveway.

Attentiveness is like washing a shape knife.

Illumination is like searching for a job or buying a house: no, no, no, no, no...Yes.

I am so attached to a clear mind I can't believe that I have it all the time.

A pure mind is a gift: the simplicity of it.

The essence of mind is as clear as the sky.

With a pure mind the whole world becomes clear.

Use whatever is helpful.

Heaven is Earth; Earth is Heaven.

Rejection is acceptance.

I'm in the midst of it.

It is restful in space.

It is being at peace in the middle of activity.

Free from thought I spring into spontaneous action like a meadow hawk.

It's like cooking rice: never peek in the pot.

It's like releasing the grip of my mind.

Why am I afraid to realize it?

There is a final insight.

It's like waiting for the punch line of a joke.

Humor works and music works also.

It's like pushing the space bar on my keyboard.

It is like calling the office on the telephone and waiting for someone to answer.

It's like a batter in the batter's box.

It is like taking a very hot bath, or shaving my head.

Was Tarzan close to it?

It's like meeting another car at an intersection.

It is like, "Checkmate!"

It's like getting hit in the face with a cream pie.

Sometimes to look into another person's eyes is enough.

It's like a river at flood stage.

My mantra is, "I am one with all things in the universe."

Every time that I walk right up to it, I don't walk up to it at all.

It's like being on vacation.

It's like a distant sound and not being able to put a name on it.

It's like a cautious robber at the wayside.

It's like taking care of a sick child.

It's like being a fool.

It's like defining Good, or Justice, or Beauty... or Love... or Truth.

It's like channel surfing.

It's like writing my own book.

It's like *The Eye That Never Sleeps* written by Dennis Genpo Merzel.

It's like losing my mind.

It's like having my thoughts fall off a cliff.

It's like baby-sitting.

It's like an empty field.

It's like a matador facing a bull, or like Socrates and a Sophist.

Silence is beautiful

It's like Sisyphus repeatedly pushing his boulder to the top of the mountain, and then watching it roll down to the bottom.

It's like geese riding the wind, or like a seagull practicing its diving.

It's like being in the desert.

It's like a robin looking for worms.

It's like living in the Garden of Eden, or being baptized, or swimming under water.

It's like falling in and out of bed.

It is like untying a knot in a piece of string.

It's like little children playing make-believe.

True clarity is open to all.

Just relax and it naturally opens up.

There are so many levels to cross; and yet, only one step is needed.

What is the most precious thing that I possess?

BIBLIOGRAPHY

Confucius and the Confucian Classics. Ed. Rev. A. W.
    Loomis. Tran. Rev. James Legge, D.D.
    San Francisco: A. Roman and Co. c.1932.

Dhammapada. Rendered by Thomas Byrom.
    Boston: Shambhala, 1993.

Fung Yu-Lan. *A Short History of Chinese Philosophy.*
    Trans. Derk Bodde.
    New York: MacMillan, 1948.

Huang Po. *The Teachings of Huang Po.*
    Trans. John Blofeld.
    Boston: Shambhala, 1994.

Kokushi, Muso. *Dream Conversations.*
      Trans. Thomas Cleary.
      Boston: Shambhala, 1994.

Lao Tsu. *The Way of Life According to Lao Tzu.* Trans.
      Witter Bynner.
      New York: G. P. Putnam and Sons, 1972.

Okakura, Kakuzo. *The Book of Tea.*
      Boston: Shambhala, 1993.

Spinoza, Baruch. *Works of Spinoza,* Vol. II. Trans. R. H.
      M. Elwes.
      New York: Dover Publications, 1951.

ABOUT THE AUTHOR:

Robert Tosei Osterman has been a practitioner of Zen since 1986. He was ordained a Zen Buddhist monk in 2004. He currently lives a quiet life in rural Wisconsin.

A portion of the author's royalty for this book is being donated to Ryumonji Zen Monastery, Dorchester, Iowa 52140